New and
Selected
Sorrows

New and Selected Sorrows

Goran Simić

STACK
BOOKS

Smokestack Books
1 Lake Terrace, Grewelthorpe
Ripon HG4 3BU
e-mail: info@smokestack-books.co.uk
www.smokestack-books.co.uk

New and Selected Sorrows

Author photograph: Kemal Hadzic
Cover image: Luna Luna

ISBN 978-0-9927409-9-3

Smokestack Books is represented
by Inpress Ltd

for the Scottish composer
Nigel Osborne

CONTENTS

My Accent

I love my accent, I love that wild sea
which attacks my weak tongue.
It doesn't reside in the morning radio news
as much as in the rustle of the job-offer flyers
stapled to the street poles.
In my accent you can find my past,
the different me who still talks with imagined fish
in a glass of water.

My grandfather was a fisherman
and I grew up on a dock
waiting for him to come back.
He built a gigantic aquarium when I was born
and every time he brought a fish
he named it immediately by some word I had to learn
until the next came… next came… next came.
I remember the first two were called 'I am'
and after that the beauty of language came to me
through the shining scales.
I learned by watching the aquarium
and recognizing the words by the silent colours.
After returning home
my grandfather would spend whole nights
making sentences by combining the fish
who would pass each other.
It's how I learned to speak.

I left the house the day my grandfather went
fishing for a black fish he was missing
and never came back.

Now I am sitting in the middle of my empty room
as in an aquarium
and talking with the ghosts of the fish
I used to recognize as words,
talking with the shadows floating
over the flyers ripped off street poles.

'I love my accent...
I love my accent...'
I repeat it again and again
so as not to ask myself:

Who am I now?
Am I real or just the black fish
my grandfather failed to catch?

An ordinary man

I am an ordinary man with ears of ordinary silk
and I speak only with a voice I've heard somewhere,
a voice like an echo.
I've given up blunders:
that leg of mine intact in the sky was
an ordinary crutch made of rosewood
and when I talk about flowers
my voice smells of earth
in which blind moles delve.

I've given up blunders.
I know that rifle ranges, crowded at night with sad people,
were invented only because of the law
by which they protect somebody
from my gunpowder dreams.

I admit I sometimes start to cry at night
but so do the others.
I've met many people and they all resembled me.
Some hid in the bodies already used as corpses,
the others hid in corpses in which
an attentive ear can recognize a breath.
But they all had obedient eyes. And they liked dogs.
I've entered maiden's rooms filled with snow,
I've sniffed empty bedclothes and imagined
black stockings removed from maiden legs
only for me.
But so did the others.

Sometimes from the window I notice breadcrumbs
in the hair of women I once loved.
But they are now someone else's women
and now that's somebody else's bread.
I am an ordinary man and it's clear to me:
whenever I was born I'll die young.
I die every day and I am not afraid anymore
when in passing I notice my pale face
going by the other way.
That is why I sleep slowly.

Only sometimes
I am sad and begin to cry
though I don't know why.
And I feel sorry I am crying
and sorry I don't know why.

But so do the others.

Airport

We are flying. I tell you, we are flying
and I smile to you deep in the womb of the airplane.
I offer you a wallet in which you will find
only dusty tickets.
I present you with white gloves,
an axe whose blade you can use as a mirror.
You keep silent, staring at
the stewardess in the army uniform.
You are silent, silent.

Sooty angels knock on windows selling medals,
necklaces of nickel-plated stars.
Handsome devil revolutionaries
offer us flocks of tamed clouds,
old goddesses trade their former splendor
and you hide behind a newspaper.

What year is this?
Do you remember your license plate number,
do you know the number of this flight?
We are flying, I tell you,
we sacred swine are flying,
we ordinary heroes you can meet at the circus box-offices.
We are flying, I tell you,
though it looks to me
like we haven't even left the runway.

Passport borders

They returned my passport.
A faceless man just came to my door
and brought me my passport,
still damp from last year's snow.
Your legs, he told me,
stick out of our trousers too much
and your head thinks more about the victims
of a future war than our past and our flag.
That's what he said
and ran down the stairs while
broken teeth and seagull feathers
fell out of his pockets.
He took away even his shadow.

He returned my face
that had been sitting in the police files for years,
my smile from the time when I believed
that wisdom was as big as a travel bag.
He returned my passport
when I'd forgotten I ever had it.

Perhaps he didn't know that I often travelled at night,
that my skin was full of odors
of continents unknown to him
and my room full of things meaningful only to me:
I brought an icicle from the North,
fire from the South,
a candle from the East,
wind from the West,
and I didn't have to justify to anybody
my simple need to avoid maps and routes
already travelled by those who came before me.

He returned my passport.
He brought back the borders
and changed me into a simple traveller
who will be forced to compare himself.

Perhaps that's why he returned
my passport.

Who's that waking me up?

Prisoners walk in circles. It's morning. It's dark.
Step by step they free themselves from life-long fears.
Because of them I wake up
frightened that I don't know yet
where the wrong side starts.
I do notice that my room gets smaller every day
and I often hear masons working in the wall.
Where is the limit of shame?
Whose bed am I lying in?
Sleep, Goran, sleep.
The night exists just to prevent you
from meeting me.

Years go by, drinkable, but full of fear.
I am more and more inclined to fall. Have I fallen already?
God sometimes knocks on my frozen window
and I don't let him in because
he has the eyes of a prisoner and always asks: Why?
As if I knew.
I just half-breathe humbly and die the other half
looking for the place where the exit door used to be.
Sleep, Goran, sleep.
Prisoners do not exist.

Where are you going, father, in your slippers?
It's morning. It's dark. Sleep!
Leave that empty revolver case,
and stop walking like prisoners walk.
We're tame people and do not ask me anything.
I often meet you in myself and you always ask: Why?
As if you didn't know what's going on in your head
when you ask me on which side
medals should be worn.

To whom have you rented your son,
I ask you quietly so that mother won't hear,
blind but ever wakeful for I know she will ask me:
What's going on outside? As if I know.
Therefore, sleep, Goran, sleep
as sheep, butterflies,
tame people sleep.

Just so

So, I was in a madhouse and understood everything. I did.
I listened to harmonious sounds of heavenly microphones
and loudspeakers of hell,
to the rain drumming on distant suitcases
I had once left somewhere by the road.
I remember that I didn't fear anything
and was mostly afraid of that.
For months I imagined I was a skeleton
decorated with medals going
through passport control.
But even that is over and everything
becomes clearer to me.

I was in prison also and listened to them beating me. I did.
I don't remember the dates but my scars do.
Like the blue jaws of a shark pulled out of the sea
I bit the air and the barrier behind me.
Secretly I kept a small mirror.
My father's sad army raincoat would enter
through the wall at night and just sit in the corner
only to be chased away by guards in the morning.
But even that is over now and everything
becomes clearer to me.

Later I remitted. I settled accounts. I did.
I left my crutches in the forest
when the wind took my father's raincoat
somewhere to the sky.
I talked to my shadow, chatted with the river god,
and many trivial details are now behind me.

But because of these things I believe
I will not die in an armchair
with a cat in my lap
and a cane at hand
one day.
By the window.

To the dining car

Well, let's go and have another drink.
Let's go to the dining car while time gallops under us
like water gushing in the toilet of a train.
Let's go where sweaty soldiers sleep on empty beer crates,
to the end of the world of those who rule,
those with no more questions.

Let's step into the corridor as into a holiday dawn,
serene and meek,
let's pass by the open doors of lavatories
dragging wet shreds of toilet paper on our heels.
As we pass by we'll peep into compartments:
Look, a blue spider emerges from that man's mouth,
that child's head is strangely shaped,
look, that woman cannot bend her orthopaedic crutch,
see, thousands of gnats cover them, look, look,
and please don't mention the candle.
Don't mention the candle.

Let's go there.
We'll press our noses to the carriage windows
trying to guess where we are
but all we'll see will be our eyes wide open in the glass.
Like the eyes of dead fish belly-up on the water.
Where we're headed or whether we'll ever get off this train
will lessen in importance.

Well, then,
let's go to the dining car and have another drink,
there where the search for destinations ends.
Let's go to the bar
where the conductor's uniform swings,
where shadows of loose women sway,
where the door opens to and fro,
to and fro,
opens both ways.

I am afraid I'll change

God, I'm afraid I'll change
to become one of the faces on a family photograph
in negative. It means I'll become alien: a photograph record,
a bottle label, a can
or simply a runway built along a river.
I'll trim my fingers, cut my hair, and start thinking
the way I never thought before,
the obvious way.
It will be late when I notice the trees
which remain the same.

What if I change without being aware of it?
In the morning the sweat dripping from town monuments
I'll call dew not knowing that it isn't.
I will smell like a clown thinking of death,
I, a wine jug broken on virginal bedclothes.
Yet I won't be like that.

I am afraid I'll change.
Not because of wallpaper I'll wear.
Not because of that.
Goodness, nobody is given to choose the world.
But because the others will remain the same.
My face will humbly stand
in the line of the uncalled for
and be their leader.
And yet be one of them.

I am afraid I'll change.
It will happen for sure and there's nothing
to be done about it.
Therefore I am afraid,
O God.

A note on the forest and you

I followed you to the first tree
that spring when we were so poor
and at home we banned the words
calendar and clock.
I followed your lean shadow which ingratiated itself
to the invisible border behind which
the forest began,
cold as a military formation.

Look,
on a 100-year-old beech a sailor has engraved
his rank and the name of his darling.
What is their love like now
and does the name still compare to the rank?

In the bark of an oak, bullets glitter like a constellation
made by somebody learning
how to handle a gun.
Whose face did he imagine while aiming?
Did his finger sweat while reaching for the cold trigger
where the beauty of persuasion
was turning into noise?

Even that fallen tree
resembles the tree behind our house
in which my grandfather used to hide his gun
and I pretended not to see.
Until both my grandfather and the gun disappeared.

I followed you to the first tree
that spring when poverty seemed to you
as visible as a uniform.
Then the forest surrounded you
and your voice turned into a shot.

Have you seen my grandfather
who is wandering through the forest
with an army of shadows
perfectly unaware of the meaning of calendar and clock?
Is the ghost of a sailor
now engraving your name into a tree?

I am trying to unravel this
in the constellation of bullets
in the bark of the oak
behind which begins the world
where I don't know how to belong.

Curtains

I wake you up in the middle of the night and say:
I'm having an interesting dream. Let's dream it together.
You just smile and turn onto your other side.
I just want to tell you
that on the corner of our bed,
our untouchable state with a sheet for a flag,
an Aboriginal and a Laplander sit
and leaf through a book on Indians.
I want to tell you
that our blanket resembles more and more the thick curtains
I drew over the windows to separate us from the street.
I want to tell you that for years now
I have been unable to sleep
watching you smile in yours.

Candle of the north

Take me to the beach, my darling,
let us walk over pebbles that don't smell of fish from the market,
walk where a breeze lazily leafs through last year's newspapers,
through decomposed documents of long-dead blood donors.

Take me to the beach
and keep in mind that I'm scared
watching children and emigrants cross the unlighted street.
I no longer care to hide in my pocket
fingers red with the pain
of turning the radio dial all night,
looking for a programme that plays silence.
I am not ashamed of trying to think nothing, absolutely nothing.

Perhaps we might still see that hole in the sky from which
I cut out a whole constellation and gave it to you,
believing it would fit in your wallet.
Last Sunday I found the same stars in the basement
hiding amongst last year's horoscopes and newspaper clippings
about lucky lottery winners.

Take me to the beach
and walk with me over crossword-puzzle magazines
and let us listen to those crying children who are not my own
and let me just smile to people
who smile like me.

My hands are as cold as TV news, my skin as blue
as the stamp on a birth certificate.

But somewhere in a northern room
a strange candle burns and wakes me up,
a candle that I melt down,
and I smell soil when diving in my dream
to the bottom of the ocean,
looking for something that was promised to me
when I was born.

My hunting gun hangs on the wall
next to the photo of the deer
I followed into the minefield.
Every time I dream I walk to the stars
I found socks full of blood in the morning.

I know that East is easy,
that West is always opposite
and in the North lost people
sit around a single candle
to warm their cold fingers.
It is where mothers make sandwiches
already eaten by sorrow and the long wait
for better days to come.

For years I couldn't wash the breadcrumbs from my hands.
Were these crumbs from the school bags of northern children?
Those same children who need to recognize when they go home
the difference between street-lights and a wolf's shinning eyes?

They are not breadcrumbs, I console myself,
they are just the black sand falling from that place
from which I cut the constellation.
But I know this is not the truth.
I once tattooed a lamb on my forehead
but when I woke the next day it had disappeared
and only bones remained.

So take me to the beach my darling,
where every single pebble has its own rhyme,
nothing but a rhyme, with no meaning.

Adam

My name is Adam. They call me a boy.
They tell me I'll be grown-up when I can wear
grandpa's shoes and recognize the difference
between my sister's pubic hair and my own.
My grandpa was buried in his shoes long ago
and my sister locks the door
whenever she is in the bathroom. Through the keyhole
I have watched her take off her clothes
and caress her pointy breast.
I read her diary and know for whom
she puts on lipstick. She will leave me soon
and nothing will remain with which to compare.

I know only that I was a boy just yesterday.
I'm the ghost of the house today,
growing up languid as a hothouse flower,
or a lizard daydreaming of becoming a dragon.

I know why my father grabs his gun
and runs up to the roof whenever the red
police light shines through my aquarium.
He never notices that I have emptied the bullets from his gun
and I never told him I couldn't stand
the thought of him in jail for years.

I know why my mother leaves at midnight,
picked up by a driver in a black limousine.
If I told her I used her needle to prick holes in her condoms
she still wouldn't understand how much I need her at home.

They chose the wrong uniform, my grandma tells me,
when they occasionally met and fought.
Before I grow up she'll awake and rise to the radio,
the same voice on the news promising the end of the war.
Now she listens to the fairy tales I read her every night
and looks happy. I never told her that the last rent packet we paid
held the shape of her wedding ring.
She's going to leave me soon, I know it
by the way she listens to my fairy tales, asking me
to avoid the parts when flowers die.

My name is Adam and I'm still a boy.
If I go to the movies I sit next to the exit
because some man always tells me
I shouldn't listen to my teachers
when they talk about love between boys and girls.

I didn't go back to school after a teacher
pushed me into the swimming pool.
I stayed underwater until he
had a heart attack.

Outside my window sad people walk the street
and compare themselves with passers-by.
Outside people wear masks while walking dogs.
Even dogs wear masks. Outside is a mess.

Sometimes I sit in the bathroom for hours
and imagine having a shower.

They say it happens to everybody.
But it happens now only to me.
To Adam, to the boy who sits in a cage,
believing invisible bars on his eyelids
protect him from the mess
outside his window.

An excerpt from my conversation with god

I quarrelled with god all night. What a nightmare.
I almost burst into tears when I realized that we resembled
a married couple divorcing because of adultery
even though they are still in love.
Absent-minded, with the north reflected in his eyes,
he listened to the war in my voice,
to my hundreds of questions which rang like answers.
He fidgeted, scratched behind his ear, coughed,
twisted his moustache, glanced at the ceiling,
and didn't say a thing.

I showed him the circle on the finger of an old woman
who had just sold her wedding ring.
I showed him a shoe thrown onto a garbage heap.
Is it the same shoe the boy with crutches wears,
the one who is begging behind the church to buy back his
family's history?
I think I told him even shaking hands would not
persuade me that he existed. But I'm not sure.

I woke up beside an ashtray full of cigarette butts
and felt better when the hangover hit.
I think I even smiled,
like a husband who after having agreed with his unfaithful wife
on all of the details of their divorce,
damages the lift
and walks down from the hundredth floor,
stair by stair
impatient to recognize the one
who walks up.

Angels

Angels hover over the city that eats its own roads,
whose people disappear on trains. Can you hear them?
They are not the angels we remember from Christmas cards,
they don't resemble sleepy children anymore.
We live in a time of change
and everyone wears a blood-proof watch.

I am talking about angels who feel at home in police files,
about angels shaped like flies, buzzing around computers.
I swear I caught one trying to rip out my passport photo.
Another rewrote the prescription for my glasses.
I wonder less and less about the difference
between what I remember and what I see,
why I so often find feathers in my wallet
and holes in my pockets.

Angels hover and stardust falls from their wings and covers
bed frames made from Santa's sleigh,
pyjamas that smell of graveyard soil.
They bribe the morning light to look like the TV screen
and our heads become so heavy
we understand nothing but weather reports.

They no longer live among the bright clouds
and don't waste time coaxing the wind to lift
schoolgirls' skirts for fun
or decorate trees with the hats of passers-by.
No more does Cupid sport with arrows and broken hearts,
no more are yesterday's lovers today's parents.
Angels now live among the greasy clouds,
counting tardy workers and their broken dreams.
They are too busy designing uniforms
to notice the boot prints of the soldiers that remain behind.

Who knows whether a postman will recognize our fear
when he comes near our famished mailbox?
Who knows whether a policeman on night shift
will recognize the sorrow tattooed on our hands
while waving to a flock of geese leaving town?
Will a lumberjack ever understand our tears
when he cuts down the apple tree that has for a long time produced
nothing but flowers?

Yes, angels hover over the city,
disguised in the white coats of doctors
who hide their nicotined fingers, and we resemble more and more
retired firefighters wandering in new uniforms.

Their fingers kiss our skin the way spiders
kiss the strings of the guitar we left in the basement
and never learned to play. Can you hear them laughing
while writing their names on the letters we send ourselves?

On the library shelves there are no more books about angels.
There is only a big hole through which one can hear screams
and smell the smoke of burning houses. We don't talk anymore.
We just whisper, wait for our children to come back from school
with notebooks full of writing about gentle angels
and their home among the bright clouds.

This is the year of change, we whisper and smile.
We whispered and smiled about changes last year too.

Dream nuance

I am blind, I say. Then I am silent for a long time. I lie.
I look out the window: freezing children sing
under the Christmas tree and the snow is like a rainbow.
Frozen sparrows fall from the branches onto a butcher
dragging a slaughtered lamb. It is night.
A picture of a saint blazes in the stove. The airport drone
and I feel like crying. I am blind, I say, I am blind.
She is silent, absent-mindedly taps her fingers on the table.

I've forgotten, I whisper. Then I'm dully silent. I lie.
In my X-ray eyes still sparkle three shoes cast
by a horse that fled long ago. I remember well:
with a chained dog father hunted men and I
barked at birds. Hotel vacuum cleaners now roar.
It is as dark as before and the air already smells of TV sets.
Frost. Frost. Frost, I repeat.
She keeps silent, as if she hasn't heard me at all.

And so I sit silent. After all, what else can I do? What?
I am already used to traffic lights, to the skin of a chameleon,
to someone who isn't me. It's cold. The universe buzzes
above the control tower, the fish serenely chew
oxygen bubbles, the orchards smell of hay. And it is dark.
Only now and then, someone from the bottle smiles as if
everything is just a dream nuance.
Can you see me? I ask her. Can you see me at all?
                    She nods. But she is lying.
I don't care anymore. She doesn't understand me anyway.

Back door

While I watch the front door, officers with gold
buttons for eyes enter my back door and look for
my glasses. Their gloves leave the prints of their
ranks on the plates in which I find my reflection,
on the cups from which I never drink, on the
windows bending outward. Then they leave
with crude jokes about the women I once loved.

Through my back door the police enter
regularly, with rubber pencils behind their belts.
Like kisses their ears splash when they stick to
my books which whine at night like pet dogs in
the snow. Their fingerprints remain on my
doorknob when they leave through my back
door, and their uniforms fade like cans in the river.

Why do postmen enter through my back door
with bags stinking of formalin? Their heavy
soldier boots march through my bathroom and I
can hear them looking for the pyjamas hidden in
a box of carbon paper. I ask them why they need
my pyjamas and their eyes flash for a moment
with April tenderness. Then they slam the door
and the room is illuminated by darkness.

And I still watch the front door where the
shadow of someone's hand lies by the doorbell.
Someone should enter. Someone should enter soon.

Winter that lasts in the skin of women

Slowly, the snow melts.
I do not know who I am. But I know
women will give birth to pregnant daughters,
that they will plant the trees that are a forest
from the moment they sob together,
not knowing for whom.
With an axe hung from his belt, someone will stand
above beds covered by last season's leaves
and so the past will be renewed.
And I will try to guess who it is, and whether or not he looks like me
even though I have only seen my blood in a test tube.

The snow melts.
The creek bears my mother's hair ribbons,
my sister's diary and the dog collar I wore
until I learned how to bark and hide the cat's heart
beneath my black fur. If I stayed longer I would probably
see the leaves I collected for my herbarium long ago
before learning from melting icicles
that grass smells only when it's cut,
that in my temple of bones
I breathe only swaths while comparing the claws
and nails of my hundred fingers.
So I've grown.

O tell me who I am.
For a long time I lived my literary imagination.
For a long time now I have hovered over a bookshelf,
an inkless page. Too many things remind me of death,
of this planet I dare not touch.

Watching the shadow of someone with an axe in his belt
I doubt more and more.
Yes, I doubt more and more often
that the snow melts at all.

My shadow

Her fingers were in my pocket.
She checked the government stamp on my ID,
the stamp across my smiling face,
though I no longer remember what I was smiling for.
I only remember that the shoes
I didn't try on were pinching me.

She breathes under my pillow,
caresses the rabbit-fur cover of my passport.
Her breath smells of ashes,
her touch soft on my skin.
She smells everything, even my suit
on the other half of the bed
still littered with crumbs from a wedding cake.
She knows everything. The house knows her fingertips.

She has slept in my work clothes.
She has silenced my alarm clock.

Because of her I dream of darkness,
which spreads like an illness over my body.
Because of her I chew on horror
the way a shell chews its pearl.

Who will eat my breakfast tomorrow morning?
Who will tell my boss I will be late again?
Who will listen to my fellow workers make jokes?
A shadow is a poor excuse.

They know nothing about my shadow.
They know nothing about how day follows day
and I no longer recognize my face in the mirror.
They do not know my shadow shaves every morning.
And how every morning I would cut my skin
if I wasn't afraid I might see
no blood.

Climbing up again

Where are my friends, I ask you? Where are they?
I shout on the stairway while the wind whistles
through the broken panes of the entrance.
Tell me and I'll protect you with this uniform
made from my skin,
yes, me, the man with a graphite voice
and an eraser's soul.

Can you hear
the breath of the lovers who left their
chalky names in the corridors,
the shadows that giggle in the empty mailbox,
all part of that everyday ritual that protects us
from one another?
I am measured by the one who breathes most loudly,
as are you.

Don't let this miner's lamp confuse you,
the one that falls from my hand and rolls down the stairway
when I show you my dog's photograph.
There, I tell you,
greasy clouds whisper above the television aerials
and persuade you to switch them on.
Convicts selling small crucifixes knock on your door
to sell you on the beauty of death,
though you don't see it.
You listen with fear and think that I am wrong
when I claim that every day dawns dark,
from soldiers' boots thudding steps of unclear origin.

I miss my friends, I whisper to you.
Do not fear my glance above the lift alarm.
I console myself by carrying bullet cases
which remind me that I could have been someone else.

I've practiced life too long, I tell you.
I like only your ears,
which try to defend themselves while I explain
that I am climbing the stairs with a night shift of miners.

I hear the needle and thread in your sleeve,
I sniff machine oil, I feel the tailor's sweat
when I ask you to show me the way to the hill
where I was born as a bird
a long time before I learned to crawl.

Perhaps I will find my friends there,
my generation of corpses with whom I'll die
fighting for the same breath.

But you flee. I sink deeper. Deeper.
In the snow. Which remains. After you. While the wind whistles.
Through the broken. Panes. Of the entrance.

A dream

You will dream that you are sleeping
and dreaming how: you will sleepily imagine
something you will not remember anymore.

When you wake up
you will find
fragments of a broken mirror in your mouth,
orthopaedic crutches lying beneath your bed.
The day will crawl outside
as if nothing has happened.

Only later you will discover
the bloody pillow beneath your head.

Christmas tree decorations

My children and I decorate the Christmas tree.
Outside the moon howls in the eyes of a hungry dog.
I have brought from the attic a box of family ornaments.
We recognize in their reflections
our own joyful faces from past years.

The shining decoration on top is my Grandfather.
From the Russian war he brought home
just the bullet in his shoulder,
and the need not to speak
whenever conversation turned to war.
Why did he die with a smile in his face?

This other ornament is my Uncle's,
a war hero who jumped from his hospital window.
The doctors said he often dreamt
of bombs being thrown into his room.
When he died he had so shrivelled
we buried him in a child's coffin,
too small to display all his medals.

That next decoration is of another Uncle.
He was convinced that Communists
had planted a bug in his mouth,
which was why he spoke a language
of his own invention.
He died in prison after authorities discovered
his strange words sounded like secret codes.

The next bauble belongs to my Aunt.
While gathering wildflowers
with which to decorate the liberators,
she didn't notice that she had wandered into a minefield,
and never found out her husband
was not among them.

Perhaps he would have been,
if only he'd not been so fond of dancing
to the grenades clinking round his waist.

The red decoration is my Father.
At the end of the war he came home a hero,
but amid the celebrations scattered the brains
of a drunk comrade who'd tried to rape a village girl.
He'd still be in prison
if that girl hadn't been his sister.
He remained imprisoned long after his release.

This decoration, here, is my Brother.
He never learned to properly fire a rifle.
The last time he pulled the trigger
He shot a Christmas tree and died of sorrow.

This last small black ornament is Mother.
After surviving the concentration camp
she dedicated her life to lighting candles,
and washing family graves.

I stand with my children
at the foot of the Christmas tree.
There are no more decorations.
I am thinking about how nicely
the tree's trunk will burn in our stove,
as my children dream of the morning
and the presents that await them.

Tomorrow we will wake up happy.

Medals

When he returned from the war my grandfather locked himself in the attic and did not come out for fifteen days. During the day he was silent, but at night he would moan so terribly that the candles burning under the icon went out. When he finally came downstairs, my grandmother saw the face of death.

When my father returned from the war in his blood-stained coat, he spilled a heap of medals from his bag and went up to the attic without looking at anyone. During the day we compared his medals with grandfather's, and at night we buried our heads under the pillows so as not to hear him moaning and calling out to his dead friends. Come morning, my mother would put his shiny medals on the window sill for passers-by to see. But no one passed our house anymore because no one could bear the moaning. One morning we found a ghost in the coat by the bed. The ghost had my father's eyes.

It happened a long time ago. The family vault has thickened. The medals still hang on the walls and officials sometimes take them away during holidays and bring them back after they are finished with them. I wouldn't have cared if they were never returned. Only sometimes after news of the war, horrified, I noticed them on the wall. Because the only thing left from my father and my grandfather are those screams and moans, and I console myself that it is the wind scratching the dilapidated attic and beams of our simple house.

Father and bees

Now I know that my father hasn't learned anything about war.
He hasn't learned anything about bees, either.
At the beginning of World War II
he put on a uniform and went to fight against Fascism
leaving his family home and his beehives.
When the bees went wild and started attacking children,
the locals suffocated them with smoke.
After two years of the new war,
he went to the old family house
and started raising bees again.
He stopped reading newspapers,
he swears at the authorities less and less
and disappears when someone starts talking
about politics.

He sent me a jar of honey. I haven't opened it yet.

I've heard that some 10 kilometres from the old family house
4,000 people were killed and buried.
I've heard that the stench of rotting corpses
buried at the soccer field overpowers the smell of linden.
They say that nobody can sleep at night
from the detonations of the empty stomachs of the dead
that explode in the summer heat.

My father doesn't know that.
He only raises bees and sends jars of honey.

I skim through the encyclopaedias to find out
how far bees fly and do they run away from stench.
Then I start crying.
And I can't explain to my children why I forbid them
to open the jar of honey that my father sent them.
The warrior and beekeeper
who has never learned anything about the war
or about the bees.

The wall of horror

I've heard the March leaf of the calendar
belonging to the girl next door fall. For hours
she looks at her big stomach as at a wall behind
which moves a being nailed to her womb by
drunk soldiers in a camp on the other side of the
river. She stares at the wall of horror behind
which a disease begins, a terrible disease which
lives on images and silence. Perhaps she sees her
maiden dress fluttering on a pole like a flag.
Perhaps she feels the steps of the murderer in the
sound of the falling leaf, the one she will
recognize when the child starts to resemble
something she will try to forget all her life. I
don't know. All I heard was the March leaf of the
calendar fall.

The face of sorrow

I have seen the face of sorrow. It is the face of
the Sarajevo wind leafing through newspapers
glued to the street by a puddle of blood as I
pass with a loaf of bread under my arm.

As I run across the bridge, full water canisters
in hand, it is the face of the river carrying the
corpse of a woman on whose wrist I notice
a watch.

I saw that face again in the gesture of a hand
shoving a child's shoe into a December furnace.

It is the face I find in inscriptions on the back of
family photographs fallen from a garbage truck.

It is the face which resists the pencil, incapable of
inventing the vocabulary of sorrow, the face with
which I wake to watch my neighbour standing
by the window, night after night, staring into
the dark.

The beginning, after everything

After I buried my mother, running from the
shelling of the graveyard; after soldiers returned
my brother's body wrapped in a tarp; after I saw
the fire reflected in the eyes of my children as
they ran to the cellar among the dreadful rats;
after I wiped with a dishtowel the blood from
the face of an old woman, fearing I would
recognize her; after I saw a hungry dog licking
the blood of a man lying at a crossing: after
everything, I would like to write poems which
resemble newspapers reports, so bare and cold
that I could forget them the very moment a
stranger asks: Why do you write poems which
resemble newspaper reports?

Ruža and the trams

All that Ruža left behind was her weasel-fur
collar and her monthly public transit pass. The
trams were junk heaps long ago. Ruža is already
used to soft heaven, and takes long walks with
the angels. She does not need the pass anymore.
Among the shadows in her wardrobe, the only
thing real is the conductor's greasy fingerprint
on her monthly pass.

Is he still alive? Will his fingers ever touch
Ruža's fur collar again? I don't know, I don't
know. Honest to God, I don't know how to
think after a year of war.

Lament for Vijećnica

When the National Library burned for three
days in August, the town was choked with black
snow. Those days I could not find a single pencil
in the house, and when I finally found one it did
not have the heart to write. Even the erasers left
behind a black trace. Sadly, my homeland burned.

Liberated, the heroes of novels wandered around
the city mingling with passers-by and the souls
of dead soldiers. I saw Werther sitting on a
collapsed graveyard fence, Quasimodo swinging
from a mosque's minaret. I heard Raskolnikov
and Mersault whispering in the cellar for days.
Gavroche was in camouflage, and Yossarian had
already traded secrets with the enemy. Not to
mention young Sawyer, who threw himself from
Princip's Bridge into the river for pocket money.

For three days I lived in this ghostly town with
the terrible suspicion that there were fewer and
fewer of us alive, and that the shells fell only for
me. I locked myself in the house and leafed
through tourist guides. I went out only on the
day the radio announced that ten tonnes of coal
had been taken from the library cellar. Only then
did my pencil regain its heart.

I haven't learned anything

I was engaged in studying forests and reading roots
and pretended I didn't see anything except
what went unnoticed by the others.
I knew the history of every tree,
the origins of moss,
the age of every squirrel
and I didn't even notice when the city police
changed their uniforms.

In town there were already hordes of quacks
offering recipes for eternal life in exchange for food.

Doctors were leaving hospitals and appearing on TV screens
offering the poor get-rich-quick solutions.

Incorruptible judges were going out to drink
with those they once sentenced.

Women were walking with dark circles under their eyes
and forgetting to pick up their children from day care.

Horoscopes became the most popular literature
and books of prophets were circulated as widely
as toilet-roll.

I pretended I didn't notice when my history professor
took off his hat and greeted the worst pupils
who were walking along the main street of the city
with revolvers at their belts.

I passed by the high school in which I spent years
learning about the kindness of people
and the happy endings of wars.
Refugees live there now.

I spent years there studying the dignified language of persuasion
and didn't learn anything

Not even simple words
with which I could restrain a man with an axe in his hand
measuring the maple tree
under the high school windows.
The same maple tree that for years,
by some invisible language,
persuaded me that every tree in the forest
had its name and its root and its soul.

The same maple tree
whose first leaf I glued in my herbarium
believing I was starting to learn.

Love story

The story of Bosko and Amira was a major
event that Spring. They tried to cross the
bridge out of Sarajevo, believing their future was
on the other side, where the bloody past had
already gone. Death caught them, in the middle
of the bridge. The one who pulled the trigger
wore a uniform and was never called a murderer.

Newspapers from around the world wrote about
them. Italian dailies published stories about the
Bosnian Romeo and Juliet. French journalists
wrote about a romantic love which surpassed
political boundaries. Americans saw in them the
symbol of two nations on a divided bridge. And
the British illustrated the absurdity of war with
their bodies. Only the Russians were silent.
Then the photographs of the dead lovers moved
into peaceful Springs.

My friend Prsíc, a Bosnian soldier who guarded
the bridge, watched each day as maggots, flies,
and crows finished off their swollen bodies.

I can still hear his swearing as he put on his gas
mask, when the Spring winds from the other
side of the bridge brought with it their bodies'
stench. No newspapers wrote about that.

What I saw

I saw that human feet shrink two sizes when a person dies. On the streets of Sarajevo you could see so many shoes in pools of blood. Every time I went out I tied my shoe-laces so tight my feet turned blue. God, how happy I was to return home with shoe on my feet. What a pleasure to untie the laces. What a pleasure not to lie on the street without the shoes on my feet.

Before I left the house my mother would check to see if I was wearing clean underwear. She claimed that it would be a shame if they carried me to a mortuary and found dirty underclothes on me. Better to go to a blue sky with blue feet that with no shoes.

What a shame for our family, she'd say. To be killed without dignity. God forbid!

Lejla's secret

Doctor Lejla, from the Department of Corpse Identification, went mad before the new year. She left the mortuary, scattered all their documents on the street, and locked herself in her apartment with those images of slaughtered bodies, carved ears, and eyeless heads. She responded with screams to every voice on the staircase, and at night she played her out-of-tune piano and howled like a wounded animal.

What was it she saw at the mortuary that day? Like contagion that question began to obsess her neighbours, and the secret of Lejla's madness became our nightmare. Her ghost turned our basement shelter into a workshop of horror. Some believed that she'd recognized the face of her late husband, others that she had seen a corpse sewn from the bodies of different people. The rest saw a baby in an open womb. Before long, fear of our imagination surpassed our fear of the shells. The building was soon deserted.

When they carried her away, wrists cut, on the first day of the new year, nobody came to see her off. Refugees now live in her apartment and sleep peacefully. Only the Devil still wakes to the sound of Lejla's piano.

Spring is coming

Spring is coming on crutches.
Swallows nest again in the ruins
and childrens' nappies flutter merrily on a clothesline
stretched between two graveyards. Peace
caught us unprepared to admit without shame
that we survived and that we dream about seagulls and the sea.
It brought restlessness to our Sunday suits and dancing shoes;
it settled in our stomachs like a disease.

Spring is coming on crutches.
Look, idle soldiers drunkenly roam the town
afraid they'll have to turn in their uniforms if they return home.
Look, they are carrying out a young man from the cinema
because he couldn't bear the beauty of a happy ending.
Look, the former hundred metre dash champion
sits alone at the stadium watching the shadow
of his wheelchair.
Even my neighbours don't quarrel with the same zeal
with which they were once nasty to one another.
It feels as if we woke up in our underwear under a spotlight
on the theatre stage, and we have yet to find the exit.
The peace halved us.

Spring is coming. On crutches.
The time of medals is coming,
when children from freshly whitewashed orphanages start
                    searching for family albums,
the time when big flags cover this landscape of horror
in which my neighbour, in the basement,
holds a child's winter glove in his hand. And weeps.

Repeating images

A fly walks on the TV screen where the President
announces the terrible days to follow. Behind him is a flag.
Across from that flag, a woman counts change
from the sale of the morning paper.
Her son, hands dirty with printer's ink, sleeps.
Above his head is a picture clipped from the papers
in which the President shakes hands with the boy.
It is obvious that the boy is ashamed of his dirty hands.

A few kilometres further
a driver who was once the star student at his university
takes out a sandwich wrapped in yesterday's newspaper.
Behind him a dredge loads earth onto his truck.
He wonders.
How many anthems were sung for this earth, which
stirs up dust on his bullet-drilled truck?
How many tears were shed for this simple earth
before it swallowed the last generation of fighters
and became dust?

He unwraps yesterday's newspaper
and notices how sandwiches get smaller every day
and how love passes slowly, like the wind
which blows through the broken windshield
and carries away the fresh morning newspapers
he hasn't yet managed to read.

The bridge

On the eve of the war, a foreign film crew appeared
in Ruža's village and turned her country idyll
into chaos: prefabricated shacks were assembled
and quickly painted; the skilled foreigners even
built a bridge in half a day, while embarrassed
local craftsmen looked on. The greediest
villagers became part of the history of the village
through a camera lens, taking the parts of Indians
in the Western screenplay. Pierced by arrows,
they fell from trees; shot by Winchester rifles,
they rolled down steep hills. They jumped into
rivers, fleeing cowboys, and at night they would
heal their bruises with Bosnian brandy and herbs.
One evening, the film workers took the set apart
and disappeared into the night, leaving behind
only the bridge which nobody crossed for a long time.

I watch Ruža writing a letter to her brother
who lives across that river where corpses float
like shadows. Bent over the letter, she resembles
the bridge, and even the collapsed wall of her
house looks like a film set. And I see her
covering that scar on her neck, left long ago by
some film extra who carelessly handled his bow
and arrow.

The book of rebellion

Nobody anymore remembers the secret book
that nobody ever dared mention.
Not even I who think that wisdom comes with age.
It was passed on secretly from hand to hand
like a forbidden legend that was only guessed,
and bound people with the sweet glue of curiosity
and heavy chains of caution and fear.

I took it over in the basement of the old maternity hospital
that they turned into a prison.
A man shoved it into my hands
warning me to forget his face that very instant
and making me swear that the book
would never get into the hands of the police.
I didn't even managed to tell him
how proud I was at joining.
He disappeared the same way
I disappeared the following week
after handing over the book to somebody else.
Those years of waiting for changes seemed harder than
waiting in lines for food, pencils and paper.

Now that I think about it,
I never learned the name of the book
nor were its contents ever clear to me.
Its sentences were so soaked
in the tears and sweat of former readers
that I could only make out every third word,
words like: homeland, rebellion, destruction and future.
And the title page with the author's name
had been erased by sweaty fingers
before it reached me.

Today,
when lines in front of public libraries
seem longer and longer,
it occurs to me that all of us
thousands of readers
were somehow the authors of that book.

But, the same President still rules the homeland.
He grew old in power the same way
we grow old waiting.
During statutory holidays everybody notices
the smile hovering on his face
when in his celebratory speech
he mentions the mythical Book of Rebellion
supposedly devised by
troublemakers and manipulators.

Just like the smile of somebody who
a long time ago
made a good joke
that is still being retold.

The war is over, my love

The war is over. I guess.
At least that's what the morning paper says.
On the front page there is a picture of the factory
that until yesterday produced only flags.
It is starting to make pyjamas today.

On the next page there is a report on the posthumous
awarding of medals and then there are crossword puzzles
and national lottery results
in which they regret to inform that this month
again nobody won the grand prize.

Pharmacies work all night again,
radio plays the good old hits
and it seems as if there never was a war.

I enter an old clothing shop
and on the hangers I recognize my neighbours:
There,
Ivan's coat. We used the lining for bandages.
Look,
Hasan's shoes. Shoe-laces are missing.
And Jovan's pants. The belt is gone.

But where are the people?
I run along the main street
to look at myself in the shop windows
but the shop windows are smashed
and there are only naked mannequins
that will wear new pyjamas tomorrow
according to the morning paper.

Then I run into our apartment
and look at myself in the glass
on your picture on the wall
and I don't care if I am not the same anymore,
the one who cried when they were taking you away.

You told me you would come back
my love
when the war is finally over.

The war is over.
At least according
to the morning paper.

A thick red line

A lamb escaped
and I sent the wolf to bring it back.
such lambs loiter about the forest,
and leave droppings where I like to watch the valley.

I am afraid something might happen to the wolf.
There are many fugitive lambs
very few such faithful wolves.
Years pass before you train them
not to look you in the eyes
but at your hands.

I've read in an encyclopaedia
how many people were killed in Auschwitz.
Like lambs.
Later I read a book about the same camp
but 308 victims were missing from the list.

Between those two books
my wolf treads in the deep snow
and draws a thick red line with his tail,
contentedly sniffing the air.
The spring is coming again
when the snow melts as fast as memory
and lambs feel the urge to escape.

What is left

What is left of our rebellion, which was not
mentioned in the daily papers? What is left of
our motives, remembered now only by few
of us and by those we opposed?

Just a few torn posters, the smell of ink and
shame. The colours on our flags have faded, and
we now drag along dogs and children. Only the
street is still there. The sparrows still chirp, the
same ones which flew away the moment we
arrived glowing with change.

What is left of our conspiratorial candles, which
burned so fast we couldn't count outside?
Nothing but the glow of nervous cigarettes,
comes diving into ashtrays; nothing but
gunpowder voices, echoing first grade history.
Is that all?

If each new year didn't arrive with nice cakes
and end up with dirty plates, I would think that
I'd only imagined it all, that I'd protected myself,
sparrows as witnesses, from the emptiness which
makes me watch the street, and the boy who
throws a lighted firecracker into the snow.
Under my window.

The arrival of the wolf

Welcome wolf, among our bloodthirsty sheep,
all smiling at you just to show their teeth. Do not
be confused by the greasy dishtowels you see in
place of flags. Many conquerors have passed
through this city, and none has yet succeeded in
leaving his mark.

This is the time of chaos, and roses smell of skin.
It is so dark in the corridors you creep along and
the marble has eyes clearer than your own; it will
see beautiful women collecting their hairs for their
albums. You gums gleam like medals at
celebrations, but the mirror does not tell you that
you no longer follow the deer spoor you've
sniffed through the herbarium of this city under
decaying stars.

Welcome wolf, with those funny jaws. Our
blood-thirsty sheep smile at you from the windows,
for you are not the wolf we fear. You are but a
shadow of the wolf that is following you.

Someone winds the clock after you arrive, and
wakens the moment you fall asleep, hurrying to
seal up the window through which you could see
the forest. Mice will eat your documents because
they are not afraid of anything. They do not care
about the draft at your door, nor about
the shadow of the murderer above your bed.

These are turbulent times, and you are but a wolf
from a textbook, a stuffed fur on the wall of a
hunting lodge, in this town
that no longer resembles the other towns you have
passed through.

I was a fool

I was a fool to guard my family house in vain
watching over the hill somebody else's house shine,
and, screaming, die in flames. I felt no sorrow and no pain
until I saw the torches coming. The next house will be mine.

If I wasn't somebody else, as all my life I've been,
I wouldn't say to my neighbour that I feel perfectly fine
upon seeing his beaten body. I should offer my own skin
as a tarp. Will the next beaten body be mine?

I was a fool. I love this sentence. Long live Goran and his sin.
There is no house or beaten man. There is no poetry, no line,
there is no war, there are no neighbours. There's no tarp made of skin.
But there's a pain in my stomach as I write this. It's only mine,

this sentence, the one I swallowed, whose every word
is each of the flames I saw, every scream a sword.

Midnight in the orphanage

War is the beast that lives on a dusty television screen.
The TV's off. There is no war. It happens now to others.
My mother is a burnt house. Her ghost was last seen
cursing a lot of soldiers and the few remaining fathers.

Dad is late again. He knows where I am, I guess.
Maybe he missed the train. He'll surely catch another.
I hug myself like a pillow. I'll love myself less
now that I'm my own goodnight kiss, my own goodnight mother.

But tomorrow's Sunday. The TV will be off. Let is pass.
The soldier's grave receives a child's blessing.
TV guide, Your Majesty, please don't let anyone ask:
What are you watching? Is your father still missing?

Old people and the snow

My beautiful old ones are disappearing slowly. They simply leave,
without rules, without a farewell.
They stoop down to reach a clothes-peg
and turn into earth.
Just for a day, their names
invade a modest space in the morning paper
and then withdraw before news of war.
They leave behind their diaries, their letters, and new suits
readied for their funerals long ago. They pass
like a breeze through the curtains of an abandoned apartment.
And we forget their names.
Like that of the retired captain from the ground floor
we spent half the day burying because the graveyard
was shelled so heavily we had to hide in his grave.
For three years he wrote letters to an imaginary son
and piled them in a shoebox.
Like that of a former employee of a former bank
whose diaries I bought from some refugee children just before
they started to make paper airplanes.
They were written in invisible ink.
Like that of my neighbour whose whole family had been
                massacred in the village.
who had given me the battery radio
he always had with him
before we carried him out of his basement.
He had never bought batteries or tried to switch it on.
It is snowing outside. Just like last year.

Surrounded by keepsakes whose meanings left with the old people,
I try to decipher sorrow's secret handwriting, that message which
            allows a snowman to watch
a sunrise with indifference.
Or have I already deciphered the message?
Why else would I have forgotten
to switch on the radio at a time when the news from the front
threatened to overpower my need
for letters to nobody, and diaries in which nothing is written?
While it is snowing outside. Just like last year.

At the end of the century

In my opinion
the twentieth century didn't last long,
perhaps just a few years,
enough for me to learn to walk
and to pretend that falling doesn't hurt.
That's when I also learned that
it was best to wrap wounds
in bandages made of one's skin.

I am a boy who was sitting alone for too long
in an empty classroom waiting for the teacher
who never came.
The only reminder of him was the chalk on his desk
and I kept standing in front of the empty blackboard
to daydream,
locked in the empty school.

Hidden behind the curtain,
I learned everything I learned
by peeking through the window.
I grieved for every death,
I was happy about every birth
and I commiserated with street revolutionaries
when they left with their torn banners.

The twentieth century didn't last long,
perhaps just enough for me to learn
how silence can purr beautifully
and how loneliness bites terribly.

I didn't have time to fall in love
with the pair of hands that pasted
the demolition order for the school,
with the wet eyes of the police who took me away,
with the angelic face of the female doctor
in the retirement home.

The beloved woman I've never met
lulls my children to sleep.

I haven't managed to grow old in such a way
that at least the pigeons in the park notice when I'm gone.
I happened to grow all inside,
like a watermelon
that dreamed of august for too long
and woke into a December morning.

All I have taken from life is the chalk
the teacher left behind
that seems to me as big as the universe
while I look at it through the eyes
of a boy who was only starting to learn.

A scene, after the war

for Luna and Darije

I'd never been aware how beautiful my house is
until I saw it burning,
my schoolmate told me, who had twenty pieces of shrapnel
that remained deep under his skin after the war.
He wrote me how at the airport he enjoyed
having upset the customs officials who couldn't understand
why the checkpoint metal detector howled for no reason.

I had never been aware I was a nation
until they said they'd kill me,
my friend told me,
who'd escaped from a prison camp
only to be caught and raped by Gypsies
while she was roaming in the woods.
Then they sold her to some Italian pimps
who tattooed the owner's brand and number on her fist.
She says you cannot see it when she wears gloves.

I recognized them in a small town in Belgium.
They were sitting and watching the river
carry plastic bags, cans
and garbage from the big city.
She was caressing the hard shrapnel lumps
through his shirt
and he was caressing her glove.

I wanted to say hello
and give them a jolly photograph from the times
when none of us knew the meaning
of House and Nation.

Then I realized that there was more meaning
in the language of silence
in which they were seeing off
the plastic bags down the river
than in the language
in which I would have tried to feign those faces
from the old photograph
that shows us all smiling long ago.

My dear Jorge

I have learned the beauty of your poems
and argued with your past so long
that it was too late when I noticed that my town
resembled an ashtray.
I went for a walk with you
and nobody recognized you.
Nobody.

Not the man whose daughter was rejected by the river
that couldn't stand so much beauty.
Not the pregnant woman who offered you her belly
in exchange for your cane.
Not the muddy soldier who at night secretly
pulls out wooden crosses in the graveyard
and changes their places
to make a new arrangement for sorrow.

My Jorge, the world looks different
when words do not agree to be the homeland of horror,
the horror that is easier
when it lasts for years than
when it lasts for hours.

That is why I don't talk about you anymore.
I conceal you like a hereditary disease.
The world looks different – I force myself
to say this phrase
like a prayer to protect me from the need
for your blindness brought to me in the form of verses.
My dear Jorge.

On graveyards and flowers

When I was twelve
on statutory holidays
I would secretly go to the Graveyard of Heroes at night
and steal fresh carnations from wreaths.
I would wrap them in cellophane
and sell them in the evenings
to enamoured couples in restaurants.
With the money I earned I would buy books.
At the time I thought that I would find a solution in books
to the mysterious relation between
wars and carnations.

In the meantime there were so many wars
that the graveyard spread almost
to the doors of the maternity hospital.
Nobody sells carnations in restaurants anymore
because there are fewer boys and more heroes.
Besides, fresh carnations in wreaths
have been replaced by plastic roses
because nobody has time anymore
to deal with flowers.

Now when I am almost fifty
I sometimes have the impression that
I haven't moved far from that twelve-year-old boy.
Only now
I sell my audience
those same old graves
for a few flowers on stage
beside the glass of water
and the microphone.

Open the door

Open the door, the guests are coming
some of them burned by sun, some of them pale
but every one with suitcases made of human skin.
If you look carefully at the handles, fragile as birds' spines,
you will find your own fingerprints, your mother's tears,
your grandpa's sweat.
The rain just started. The world is grey.

The guests are coming.
Some of them happy, some of them strange
with stomachs already full of strange words
they have just learned, like river and wheat.
Instead of food they still eat their own memories.
And they are not ringing. They just gently knock on your door
with a strange cat that dropped by in the backyard
from who know where.
They rain just started. It looks like snow.

The guests are in the house.
Some of them smooth as silk, some shy as a breeze.
Their fingers are as heavy as jail bars
while turning the leaves of your family tree.
And don't be surprised at hearing your ancestors talk to them
in some language you forgot a long time ago.
Even the dust on their shoes strangely recalls the dust
in your attic.
It's cold outside. Cold. Cold.

The guests are leaving. They say goodnight.
It's a long way to the next house, long as from planet to planet.
Sleeping babies in their arms just got the first lesson:
how to open the door. The rest they will learn.
They are leaving silently not to disturb your dog
watching the strange cat eating his food in the backyard.
And you are not certain if there are ghosts
or your own shadow which you left behind
long ago after you left your home
to knock on somebody's door
on some stormy night.

Differences in demolitions

In the Country where I live
when a house has to be torn down
a few workers arrive with a contract,
tear down the house in a few days and leave
and later nobody remembers anymore the names of those
who lived there until yesterday.

In the Country I came from
before the house is torn down
an armed police squad arrives
and an ambulance for someone who might want
to die grieving under the demolished roof
beneath which he was born long ago.
For months afterwards even the children avoid the place
where once there was a house
because of the ghosts of ancestors who moan
from the spiderwebs and weeds.
There the demolition ball is heavy as a curse.

In the Country I came from
the chief of the demolition squad was a certain pauper Ivo,
the man without a family but with a pistol in his belt.
For thirty years as he gathered curses
he'd take a few bricks from each demolished house.
Later he built himself a house with those bricks.

The house is still in place
because nobody lives there anymore,
because the pauper Ivo is now a simple manual labourer
in a squad of people who build houses
in the Country where I live
now.

Immigrant blues

Sorry, Mother, sorry
I didn't have the heart to tell you I died that day
when I reached the border.
Customs officials could tell you about that
if they remember the boy
with a burning suitcase in one hand
and an empty extinguisher in another.
They took everything from me,
even the flag I was wrapped in when I was born.
I could keep just what wasn't written in my
Customs Declaration:
just sorrow, memory and pain.
It's hard to live as a mouse
Once you've died as the cat.

I am lonely, Mother,
lonely as a forgotten toy in the window of a shop shut for Christmas,
lonely as the strange face in my mirror.
Only the neighbour's cat notices how gently
I am locking the door behind me
going to the bar to smile
and how hard I slam it
when I come back.

The postman thinks I am weird for paying
so much for parcels to be sent
to an unknown address
just to be returned at my birthday.
But he's just a postman
and he doesn't know much about the beautiful smell
of trains and distant countries
that the cardboard spreads for months.
He doesn't know much about
how wind caught in his raincoat reminds me
of the wind on our burning house that day
when I left.
I can still feel smoke in the air.

But Mother,
the chunk of our homeland's soil I smuggled
turned into a dust
no different from the dust on the streets
I walk every day searching for a shortcut back.
The sorrow sometimes has the shape of beauty
when the leaves start falling in the same way
they do in my memory.

Even the skin of my apartment walls became
smooth and friendly
letting me hear my neighbour crying
at the radio news from a country I never heard of.
Does he listen to me while I loudly read the letter
I sent to myself?
I don't know.
But it's a pleasant feeling not being the only mouse
in the country of cats.

If

If on the subway my hand accidentally touched yours
on that merciless ride every evening back
to my cold bachelor apartment
perhaps you would look for my shy eyes
hidden under the cap
and think:
is this the man who empties a pocket of silence into my
voice mail
a few times every day?

In the crowded train
nobody would notice me caressing a strand of your hair
that insolently smells of my pillow.
Nobody but you.
Perhaps for a moment you would think
that the world is full of lonely people
including the one
who has been sending unsigned Christmas cards
for years.

If I leaned on you tenderly
in that packed train full of tired or sleepy people
perhaps you would feel the fire in my skin
and wish to warm yourself one stop longer
on the shoulder of the shy weirdo
whose warmth reminds you of something
you have forgotten,
thinking:
the world is full of cold people with north in their bosoms
who fear touch might melt their ice.

I could have touched your hand if you hadn't got off
at the stop where you never get off.
I only needed a moment to show you
your earring
alive in my pocket all these years.
The same one I found in my bed
so long ago
before you forgot me.
But who knows if you would recognize it at all?
You would think:
The world is full of lonely people
and lost earrings.

Immigrant talk with picture
ripped from porno magazine

It's Sunday, Mary Lou,
most terrible day of the week when even empty bottles
look happy keeping company with the spiders under my bed.
They know nothing about my loneliness
shaped by wet pillows and crumbled sheets,
nothing about the emptiness that attacks me
while watching late-night programmes on TV
with one hand on a lottery ticket
and another on the glass.

It's Sunday, Mary Lou,
and I'm already tired talking with ancestors
hidden in the basket full of my dirty work clothes.
She's fake, they tell me every time I kiss your photo.
As if I don't know it.
Your long blond hair is not the same colour as your pubic bush
which obediently lies under somebody's hand. Like a lamb.
And your big breasts don't seem like the place where some baby
can get some sleep with a drop of milk between its lips.
Even your phone number
printed at the bottom of your widely spread legs
is a fake.
Or belongs to someone I don't need to call.

My neighbour's wife, the house next to mine,
seems happy walking with her kids on Sunday evening
        she can be seen in the red light district every night.
Even the tiny woman next door,
holding hands with her boyfriend who just got out of jail
says 'Hello' on Sunday.
And I pretend not to know she's wearing a big hat
just to cover the dark bruises under her eyes.
Even my landlady's dog,
fifth in the last year
walks lamely before licking my hand. On Sunday.
But my ancestors don't want to see that scene
And dive into the pockets on my work clothes.

It's Sunday, Mary Lou, lonely Sunday
When life seems different
And my loneliness has the shape of an empty bottle
keeping company with spiders and crumpled lottery tickets
under my bed.
It's Sunday, Mary Lou,
and nobody sees the moment when I put your photo
back in my wallet
to keep company with the picture of my darling
who once promised to wait for me
until I come back.

Nobody can see my pale eyes watching two photos
not able to tell which one is my darling
and which one is you, Mary Lou.

It's Sunday. Lonely Sunday.

Before the new war comes

Every Sunday we play war games to get ready for when the new war
    comes.
We know it's a fake. Our bloodthirsty imagination has the shape of
    water pistols,
but we don't gather to measure our scars but to console those cowards
abandoned in indifference
who pretend not to notice how blood became water.

White-ribbon soldiers guard the gate of the slaughterhouse
where cattle humbly enter to see for the last time
the reflections of their faces in the mirrors of the knives.

My red-ribbon soldiers guard the back where cattle leave the
    slaughterhouse
in little packages, beautifully designed like Christmas presents,
to be loaded in trucks so big that a whole army can fit in them.

Sometimes we attack white-ribbon soldiers and spray them with red.
Sometimes they attack us and spray us with white.
Than we count how many uniforms need to be dry-cleaned.

After stupid Sunday evening gets tired of us,
we brave future soldiers go to the slaughterhouse cantina
to celebrate with butchers our readiness to stand on guard.
Over the juicy steaks we sing the national anthem in spite of those
who think our blood has become a bit watered down.

Than we go home to retell battle stories to our kids
before bedtime stories about how free and happy cattle attack them,
before indifferent Monday knocks on our guarded doors.

Happy days in the mental institution

The nurse comes with a pile of pills and a glass of water.
Her sharp collar cuts the hospital air in half.
On the left lie those who pretend to be mentally ill
to avoid execution.
On the right lie those who pretend to be mentally ill
because they were chosen to execute those
chosen to be executed.

The patients on both sides don't talk,
disgusted with each other because they gnaw pillows, urinate on the
    floor,
fart in front of the doctor, and behave stupidly.

Whenever the nurse loudly concludes that some patient
must be feeling better
the mentally ill from other side shout that his condition is even worse,
claiming that the patient is closer to becoming a flower pot
than a suicide bomber.

But after midnight
when the moonlight gently moves the shadow of the barbed wire
from the outside fence to the hospital room
all the mentally ill patients
play chess so nobody wins
and punish those who feel better
with a double dose of pills.

Outside the hospital it's worse. Much worse.

Poet and his brother the general
on a hill after the war

We met on a hill on a summer night
where crickets played in the ashes of the family house
we used to call home.

He,
with a tiny hole in his chest that I made with my pen,
me,
with the scars on my skin left by his hanging medals
in the place where my heart used to be .

We promised not to talk about the end of the war curled in his
    stomach
like a dead baby waiting to be reborn,
not to talk about my shaking fingers and fact that everything I wrote
I wrote in the soil with my nails.

Look at that wild rosebush growing from the corner that used to be
    your room!
A viper coils on the plank that remains from your bookshelf!
Sparrows drink from the candle-holder on the wall
under the black frame housing the family icon.
No one can read from the record cover what music we listened to
when we learned how to dance.

When the night became dark like the words we didn't say loudly
we talked about astral power and the fact that we were too small
to compare our little lives to eternity.

Laying on soft grass that already chewed so many generations of
    bones
we were watching the sky and listening to the stars laughing at the
    vain moon
who never understood how small he would be if there is no sun.

Look at the North Star that lets you know which way to go!
There's your sign – Libra! Soon the Morning Star will appear
telling us which way to go home.
What's that red star that flies across the sky? I asked.

It's the light of the airplane carrying bones from the forensic centre
to be buried in some other country that has never experienced war.

Than we awoke
and went downhill by different paths,
without saying goodbye.

The shadow behind me

Who's behind the shadow that follows me in the middle of the night
with a face concealed in foggy fear? Each time I pass the fading street light
the shadow gets darker and longer than the slippery road in front of me.

It breathes the way a power mower gasps, stuck in a field of rye,
the way a hunter climbing uphill pants with the heartbeats of a deer.
It breathes. And breathes. And breathes.
And I fear to turn my head back,
afraid I will recognize myself.

If it's a she, it must be death.
This breeze kissing my neck is like the air
from the turned pages of the picture book I grew up with.
Morning lives in her sweet perfume.
Afternoon dozes in her soft slippers.
Night shines like dewdrops in my ears.
She bribes my imagination with a bright destiny.

If it's a he, it must be my guardian angel coming off the night shift
because his work gloves smell of hothouse compost.
He's already given my name to the flower that blooms only in the dark,
as a whole life is about the fence between
a neighbour's hot wife and her husband's nervous trigger finger.

If it's a nobody, if there is no shadow,
I am deep in trouble thinking about death again.

Mathematics of genocide

After my father peacefully died in his chair and shrank to the size of
    a boy
instead of mourning I went to Srebrenica
to search for a poem about the genocide in 1995:
8,000 men were slaughtered where mothers grow moustaches.

What I found was that 87 forensic experts and 22 miners for the last
    14 years
worked to locate and dig up the remaining 6,042 male bodies.

Officials believe they were buried
in 23 surrounding forests surrounded by 62 minefields.
The UN's File 328/03 reports claims that bodies were dumped in
    cement mixers
and then spread on the soil of 23 soccer fields to fertilize the grass.
No game is scheduled because the soccer players claim
they hear screams instead of cheers from the crowd.
Heavy rain slows the work of forensic experts
who wait for the government to reply on appeal File 1/03 asking for
the exact number of cement mixers in use at the time.

Simple mathematics tell me that if I multiply 8,000 executed men
with an average height of approximately 170 centimetres
it would come to 13,600 square metres,
almost the same size as Srebrenica.

Before taking flight back to where I came from
I spent the day walking to the epicentre of that circle of the dead
and found just a devastated ordinary house in the middle
with a burnt-out chair in front.

I sat on it and couldn't hear even my own heartbeats.
Only the crying silence in the dying battery of a calculator
made me feel as small as a boy
waiting for his father to come back.

Wind in the straight-jacket

'Until Lions have their historians
tales of the hunt shall always glorify the hunter.'

African proverb

1

I got tired of victimizing myself.
Empty perfume bottles overgrow
the pile of my mistakes
and a gigantic pen with its lame heart overpowers
my simple need to record
my little self.

I got tired of punishing myself,
of apologies because the pigment of my skin can stand
only moonlight,
tired of myself looking like a dog,
howling like a wolf,
hidden in an immigrant services file.

Banned book covers inhabited me in the form
of paper plates in the hands of Sunday park protesters.
I turned into kitsch,
a sweet monster who no longer hides a wedding ring
made of barbed wire.

I was ashamed because I allowed bank clerks
to tune their beggar-producing machine
to my blood pressure,
because I let my sorrow be measured
and packed in the same colourful boxes
left unopened under
last year's Christmas tree.

It was nobody's fault but mine,

The maple tree started drying after I engraved the name
of my forgotten homeland.
Now I am collecting dry leaves for my pillow-case,
for my ancestors who still bribe me with ampoules of blood.
My back turned to my chest,
the basement ceiling bent my spine
into a hunch.
I buy shoes in the children's department
and can't remember how to stand tall

when bullets fly
or the difference between soldiers and heroes.

I got tired of the whispers I was sending myself
from countries I never memorized,
from cities that taxed me because my eyes were too big,
from beaches where old mocking turtles
walked over a new old man covered with sand.

In those whispers
there is no return address,
no name.
Just the sound of a roaring garbage truck in the distance,
grinding perfume bottles like an anthem,
there, a few blocks away,
at the place where my sorrow starts.

2

What did I miss before I was born?

Not much it seems to me,
nothing that didn't repeat itself in the same shape.

The way mothers incessantly curse the funeral home apprentice
who sits idle at the Maternity Hospital gate
eating toast with black milk.
The way the chicken obediently goes into the coop
dreaming of the moment when a peacock will emerge from
an egg-shell in full bloom, bravely stepping
in front of the hand groping for the egg.

I am talking about the millions of shells who chew
their own brains for years, counting on the day
when a little pearl will shine on the neck of a fairy-tale queen.
Before the same queen all oceans turn into mirrors.

I am talking about my small hands
that worked for years to place a heavy metal door
in the window's place,
so I could peep at the world through its keyhole.
The same world I helped to shape the way I dislike
so I could puke on it whenever I want.

Before nightfall I draw heavy drapes
because of the mad sniper who has been active
since the war that started before I was born.
He simply shot at ordinary and contented people,
at policemen disguised in preachers' robes,

at war veterans that manage kindergartens,
at politicians disguised in postmen's uniforms,

hidden deep in the womb of the red cloud
above my scared town.
He aims at street signs named for heroes
but the streets are covered by
blood-thirsty pigeons' bodies.

He's not me. Still, I am not suspected.

Even neighbours reported seeing me looking happy
while listening to a lullaby of metal rain
tap on the roof
and pretending not to know that the sound comes
from the cocoons falling from the cloud.
the same cocoons I will obediently broom
from my doorstep.

3

I kept my birth secret
and I never used to recount things I could express
only with tears.
As a butterfly larva in nappies, I never managed to fly.
Instead, it crawled blindly obedient to the mirror
to became an ugly spot,
the eye that looks at itself.

My imagination was born from my simple need
to be silent instead of crying
because silence alone has the colour I need
to paint myself,
which finds no place on the hardware-store's palette.

How many times the Coast Guard stopped me from
swimming deep down toward the bottom of the ocean.
They begged me to give up
because there is nothing there but the moist darkness
but I would always swim underwater
in search of something promised to me
that belongs to me
which I have never truly defined.

That something that became my goal
was perhaps already registered
in my skin
in the form of bruises from the golden sandbars
while I was swimming deeper and deeper,
in the fishes' bites selfishly chewing the eternal darkness,
in my own failure to breathe my own breath again,
under the mask
in my smile.
After defeat I swim back up to the silent beach.

Who knows,
maybe I was right to marry the silence,
because my scream became my lover
who doesn't see the difference between a fishing boat
and a submarine,
who doesn't care if I breathe black water

or white air.

4

No, it wasn't me
the one who would leave the house at dawn
dressed like a fisherman
going north to reconcile clever, rebellious salmon
with thousands of blood-thirsty lures
and returning home with canisters full of oil in my hands.

It wasn't me,
who would shake desert sand
from shoes made of polar bear fur.

I was born on the tarp in the military warehouse
and a flashlight was the very first star I saw.

Perhaps I looked in the wrong direction
and learned too late that only losers have a right
to celebrate
and that headaches are what remains for conquerors,
for fear of those who celebrate.

On my first trip from clinging to my mother's skirt
to wearing my father's military backpack
I was told: the safest way to go on a crocodile hunt
is to wear crocodile-skin boots.
My pointer finger is still sweating while throwing
celebratory firecrackers into the refugee camp,
while I sniff kerosene under the vulture's wing
and read horror on the lips of the stewardess
who smiles like a pregnant woman before take-off.

But I was never the one
who went north to chop down ancient trees
to carve an old pulpit.
God is my witness.
If any witness remains
at the end of the day.

5

So many times I moved from place to place,
that I don't even remember my first address.

I remember the cities because of the train tickets
and continents because of the stamps in my passport.
I don't even carry anything else in my suitcase
but city and road maps.
I don't even get surprised anymore when the suitcase bites me
when I try to close it.

I live in the flight attendants' fake smiles
as they suspiciously eye
the plastic rose in my hand.
I drink the train conductors' politeness
when they ask me about my face's scars.
From a plastic plate I eat somebody else's bitter bread,
its country of origin written on the bottom of each slice,
which will eat me before I reach my stop.

My camera resists capturing the sunny landscapes,
my pen is dead to describe
nameless stops and faceless people.

A pocket flashlight is my guide
when thinking of my true love, who agrees
to live in my imagination.

Behind me blue snow falls from the sky
on the streets that I have just passed.

In front of me hotel rooms still devour the bones of lovers
who left with new dreams.

Strangers pronounce the name of the country they come from
like they are pronouncing
the name of a terminal illness
one dies from only in front
of a blank TV screen.

Strangers' voices sound like telephones that never ring
in new hotel rooms,
e-mail messages appear on the computer screen
as swallows
on the roof of the old family house.
The same swallows turn into storks
after patiently waiting for years on the frozen chimney
then leaving
for some other roof.

Every foreigner dies in a dream with the
old country's anthem
stuck in his throat like a fishbone,
dies with wide-open eyes
too small to take in new landscapes,
to wake up in a cold silence
after the pillow starts smelling
of the flag bleached by rain
and wind.

I am also one of those in search of home,
in search of the warmth of my mother's womb.

In search of
my first address.

6

When you left the bar

only your frozen gloves remained in my pocket.
I pretended nothing was left of you
except your lipstick on the glass
that morning will eat like breakfast.

Only the barman knows why he showed you
the exit,
only the waiter knows why you left him a condom
instead of a tip,
only I know how long I kept your gloves
in my pocket to make them soft and tasty, like ice cream.

I shouldn't drive

with your gloves on the wheel,
I shouldn't present you with a bracelet made of my hair,

I shouldn't notice the moment when the bear tattooed on my chest

bites your hand stretching its golden claws.

I could guess,
your wallet will knock on my door one day
to tell me that you were stolen
and liberate me from accusing myself
of never giving you a chance.

7

When I fall in love for the first time
I promise to donate my organs
to anyone who believes that death happens
only to those who wander from oneself to somebody else,
like food in the market that moves
from shelf to shelf.

My brain could extend the life of some old man
who believes
that there is a difference between the brain rotting from cancer
and the brain already infected by life.
It could be of use to some suicide beginner
to make another try,
or to some young preacher punishing himself in a cell
whenever his imagination overpowers the rules.

My liver is my cellar
in which the smell of the vine lives in forbidden relationship
with a young woman ready to taste her own skin.
It may be useful to someone who never tasted shame
in front of a Red Cross kitchen,
in a long line of those who believe that food eats
those who don't prepare it themselves.

He must be used to sorrow and doubts
that make love constantly,
their pregnancy in the shape of tobacco smoke.
My liver might explode like a balloon
if the new owner starts baby-talking it
after yesterday's storm comes again from the past.

That room is too small for one and too big for two.

My skin is like a map,
a battlefield where gentle fingerprints fight
with the bruises of a club.
Only I, hunter,
can read the fear in the runaway's roar,
can read from my skin why I am going
to hunt
with a gigantic pen on my shoulder
and a plastic gun in my pocket.
Out of my skin I never manage to make the flag
adapt to the hundred colours of the belt
I purchased from the retired hangman.

My skin could easily be used
as a patch for the scars on someone's cheek

but I don't see any woman who would press her lips to it

without feeling that the kiss already happened
a long time ago.

My heart could easily be placed in the chest
of some young man
ready for rebellion
but inexperienced in loss.
Unless that lucky man quickly learns
how to compare mystical bits of the new heart,
already blue from ink,
with the bits from an old wall clock
grinding hours into minutes.

But who would desire that kind of heart
already infected by love?

8

I embrace you so tight
that drops of ink appear on your skin.
You hug me back and watch
a drop of orange juice glide down from my chest
making a road like a scar.

You claim that your skin is a never-ending desert

stretched before the masters of caravans.
You comfort me
my face acquired the shape of a camel
only because of your imagination.

How horrible it must be to define
something that doesn't exist.

How wonderful it is to be protected
by the cage of words
soaked with the religion
of the deaf and blind.
In the homeland of
stupid, careless question marks
that will survive the desert even without ink
and a drop of orange.

9

If we stay in bed today
and don't go to morning Mass,
what will the exuberant Sunday morning think,
watching us through neighbour's windows
as we shamelessly breathe into each other's faces?

What will the alarm clock say,
breakfasting lost minutes on the bedside-table
just before I glue your eyelids' dark trace of night
to my hungry lips?

What will the suicidal roses say,
when you don't show up in the garden
with scissors
while I leave the impression of my palm lines
on your breasts?

What comment will the street make,
that same street that already forgot your
dead husband's walking shoes, your sorrow,
and the rotting plate number of the hearse
in the junkyard?

If my embrace looks like a nest to you,
if our bellies get tattooed by sweat
and refuse to separate,
what will the confused church door say,
that threshold you crossed only once in your wedding dress,
but so many times in black?

What will the people who consoled
you for years say,
what will the priest say when he doesn't see you
on the widows' bench
but finds some other black dress
already there?

They will forget us as soon
as new gossip gets old
and some new woman in black
sleeps through morning Mass
wrapped in her lover's skin like a baby
who doesn't know the difference between a nappy
and the flag.

As long as I love you,
who cares
what they say?

10

There is a wind that bows to the government
by flapping the flag
in front of the Parliament building.

There is a wind that runs through the gut
of the steel plant,
gnawing at hungry workers
and exiting through the chimney
like a black angel of smoke.

There is a wind that blows
in front of a pauper's house
where a mother hangs freshly washed clothes
on a line
before the factory's smoke
settles on her children's white shirts.

There is a wind that tears an umbrella
from the hand of a retired factory book-keeper
and deposits it
at the door of a woman
waiting for her husband to come home from the plant.

There is a wind that blasts through the pub door
quivering the blouses of girls
who simply smile at the bar
only on the workers' payday.

There is a wind that shamelessly lifts
the skirt of the steel plant supervisor's wife,
holding her husband's hand
as he informs the workers
that the plant's about to close.

There is a wind
that smothers the sound of children weeping
in the corner next door
as they pack their toys in moving boxes that will get smaller
each day, like bad memories,
when they abandon the apartment.

But there is also a wind that spoke
in your voice, warm wind,
when you dragged me from the pub,
brought me home,
and washed the plant's thick metallic
smell from my body.

That wind told me that you love me,
and it's the only wind
I would like to name after you.

11

My beloved wife, where are you going
so early in the morning
with a black rose in one hand
and a shovel in the other?
Judging by your frozen smile
it seems that watering the hyacinth,
choking on the smell of gasoline for days,
is not on your mind,
nor saving wallflowers suffocated by exhaust.

The road in front of our house eats itself.
It has morphed into a cloud that now spews pebbles
onto our small, shy roof.

My darling, I am going to bury you
in our garden,
so I won't have to look for you
in others,
where you'd get devoured and digested
in the bowels of military trucks.

These are the same boys who,
until yesterday,
had their friends' names inked on their shoulders.
Now they tattoo their ranks.

My beloved, do not leave the house.
It is a dear grave.
Within its walls the aroma of brewing coffee
blends with the smell of baking bread,
and the cigarette smoke
kissing the inside of the window
rises from the basement,
where Grandpa reads measuring tape and counts
how much we have lost.
God bribe us with silence, again.

There is nothing to see outside
but the shining eyes of strangers.

I only ask you to stop those workers' boots
that keep marching
from our bedroom to the children's room
and back.
I am afraid the children will wake up
too early for school,
only to find their teacher
in the classroom crucified.

12

After my old neighbour sold his house
even after the real estate agent assured me the new owner
is a retired angel,
I didn't sleep much.
Don't trust the agent,
the empty fishbowl was telling me.
Don't believe in angels who purchase old dreams,
a long-abandoned birdcage was singing to me.

Is he a soldier on his last mission
doing nothing but closely watching me through the window
with the rifle on his lap, the way I watch him
hidden behind curtains?

The light bulb in front of his house, always shining,
was the only proof of his presence.

Nor did my neighbour show up after I hired masons
to build a high brick wall between our houses.
In rage I even added barbed wire.

The wall didn't keep his moles
from eating the carrots
in my garden,
didn't stop his crows
from devastating my cornfield,
didn't stop
his bugs and butterflies from invading
my neglected rose garden.

The light bulb in front of his house never stopped shining,
feeding my nightmares.

He must be a war criminal hiding from justice,
he must be a human trafficker,
or at least a drug dealer,
I was thinking for years,
watching the light bulb shining
like my imagination.

The wall still guards me
from I can't remember what
and I get scared whenever I wonder
what would happen to my soul
if that bulb went off
leaving me to talk with the empty birdcage
and fishbowl.

13

If I don't come back from my Sunday night walk
the cleaner will bring my black suit,
FedEx will deliver my new white shirt,
our poor neighbour will set
my shining shoes at our door,
as usual.
The grocery store-clerk
will deliver boxes of frozen food,
the liquor store-clerk will bring
a selection of the wines you used to love,
the hairdresser and nail artist will seduce you
talking about happy marriages in harlequin novels
and will never tell you that I've tipped them in advance,
the jewellery shop owner will praise
your slender, artistically-shaped fingers
and every week you will find in letterbox
the antidepressants, and the little bag of cocaine,
your doctor never fails to supply.

But unless my paycheck doesn't appear
in the letter-box next month
I wonder if you'll ever notice that I never came back
from the walk I went out for
so long ago.

14

You bought me shoe-laces at the flea market
the day matches became more expensive
than dynamite.
They were too long, so I shortened them
and from the remnants I made two rings.

One for our engagement,
another for our wedding.

If I had known that my murderer would tie
my hands with the same short shoe-laces
I would have forged the ring
from my tooth's golden crown.
Then my murderer, with his finger
on the trigger,
would remember his own wife
he had proposed to with heavy military shoe-laces,
before he married the uniform,
and before he faced his empty eyes
in the reflection of my golden tooth.

The day I married you I dreamt about angels
guarding our door.
The morning they took me
I dreamt that the same angels
turned into spiders crawling
across the wall calendar
eating months and years for breakfast.

Who would have known
they would go for lunch through that dingy entrance
where long ago my golden tooth lay,
and come back from the same darkness,
quietly,
like crossing the calendar's black line
between Thursday and Friday.

Who would guess
that they would make their web
out of shoe-laces
to watch another sunset,
complaining that the shoe-laces' shadows
get shorter and shorter from one year
to the next
and shinier
than the wedding band.

15

Warm me up in your stomach
before I notice your pimples soaking the morning light
from my liver spots,
before a messenger from above
leaves the ice-cube tray on your doorstep,
before you learn to sing silently.

Warm me up before your bathroom mirror
soaks you and spills you
at the nursing home's gate,
before your mother
gets you back in her stomach.

Before your passion became incurable illness.
Before your breath became measurable
by the size of my liver spots.

16

Those lights in the sky
are not stars from unreliable textbooks.
They are the lamps in front of
the refugee centre.

There, the suicidal, preachers, and the rich
eat the same dinner
and politely smile at each other over a spoon
sharp as the knife.
They have easy conversation, complaining about airplanes
that frequently fly too high
and only occasionally crash.

The pilots' wings have been clipped
and they walk awkwardly now, like chicken.
Washed-up heroin kings now sell soil
to politicians
who monopolize people's desires
and curse the bygone rock stars
plastering concert posters on election billboards
and selling tickets for shows
cancelled last century.

Diabetics mercilessly fill their stomachs
with food that used to be forbidden,
cardiac patients are regulars
in the red-light district
where virgins serve cheap wine
poured in condoms.

No one is thinking about how to patch the big hole
in the middle of the united flag after
a satellite ripped through it
on its way to some invisible planet.
Nobody even remembers the symbol
that flag used to carry with dignity,
the New Republic of Refugees
functioning perfectly with no one showing a need
to be recognized by anyone.

All that's missing in that perfect nation of the dead
is fear.
Fear that perfection will vanish someday,
like distant planets vanishing by the minute,
fear that someday they will have to come back
to earth
as refugees.

17

We are riding a tandem.
Nobody knows
who is steering or
who is pedaling.
Our burning heads dive into the dawn
while our fragile spines pretend
to be strong whenever our flat tires drive
over the hungry soil
that has composted so many generations of students
who believed that
only dust determines the difference
between the colours of the flags.

If I ask my mother to wash my dark clothes
in the sea
for as long
as the pains in my stomach have lasted,
if you ask your mother
to wash yours
for as long
as you've harboured your suspicion,
we would wear only pure white,
the cheap fabric ready to embrace
newborns and the dying alike.

We are riding on the same bicycle
toward the sunrise
pretending not to see children going to school
with backpacks reeking of fuel
and no longer holding fairy tales.
They wave to us with handkerchiefs
soaked in fear
upon seeing one body with four hands and four legs
driving toward the place
that used to be the homeland of lullabies.
We wave back with our helmets
too small to carry our heads.

We are riding the same bicycle
through devastated villages,
past houses built with bricks
that an invisible hand brought
from the Berlin Wall.

A man waves to us with a death certificate,
a woman waves to us
with nappies so transparent that we can read
the expiration date
on the faces of future mothers.
The crib and the death-bed
seem the same
when the desert wind starts blowing sand
in our face
with no homeland
and with no knowledge of the people
riding the bicycle.

This is not the end of the ride
we used to take every day, I tell you,
wiping the cement-heavy sand
from your shoes.

This is just the beginning of the day, you tell me,
wiping the dark clouds from my face.

And we get off the flat-tired bike
to go in different directions
wondering on the way to our devastated homes:
did we ride some stationary bicycle together
in some foreign country?
or was the bicycle as real
as we are?

18

The owner of the flower shop swears to God and the police
he didn't think even for a second
that the young man who entered his shop
could be a suicide bomber,
the one who thanked him for wrapping 23 red roses so nicely
and even left a good tip.

The ticket seller at the bus station averred
that the striking young man was extremely polite
and even held a second flower bouquet
as he boarded that bus.

No more witnesses were found
after the police took the corpses away,
shy of their destination,
to the city morgue,
and after the metal scraps of the bus finally made it
to the junkyard.

Only a red rose petal
floating on engine oil pooled in the cratered asphalt
remained as a witness.

What gives me the right to search for the meaning
of 23 red roses
is the same thing that keeps me from thinking
about that young man as a dark messenger
since I just missed that bus,
late as usual
after watering my rose garden too long.

19

My generation never had the patience
to grow old decently.
Some of them would rather believe
that all sheep are black in the darkness
than that every wolf is colour-blind.

Some of them died after realizing
they didn't even have time to cry over
the puddle of blood in their parents' biographies
not needing to disturb mute school books
in the teachers' stomachs,
not wanting to confront stage microphones
that proclaimed themselves human.

The moment they believe
that roses in the garden never cease
to be roses even when they stink
they turn a blind eye
as their kids search the internet
for second-hand guns.

They happened to live in the time when graveyards
became people's favourite picnic spots,
lit up all night,
when madhouses became power stations,
when hashish started to smell like incense.

They stepped back
with books about vanished tribes in their hands
and became the colour of a park bench.

For four years I wandered as well
through the morgue
pulling doctors' sleeves in vain,
shouting that the cardiovascular machines are too old
for any conclusions about my heart.

Then I was thrown out
to wander the dead city.
What an idiot I was.
I could have spent a few more years
in the secure, air-conditioned morgue.

20

I fingerpaint in a book with my daughter.
Her index finger is a spring of life
reanimating vanished birds, little reptiles
and rabbits ready to run.

I am telling her a story about
how some winter long ago I went
with my grandfather to hunt
a gigantic, wild wolf who used to attack
all the weaker animals in the forest.

In real life I've never seen these different creatures I'm bringing to life,
she says.
Were they eaten by that wolf
you and your grandfather didn't manage to kill?

Then with my sleeve I hide my own index finger
still frozen since it trembled on the trigger that winter
and ask myself again,
was I wrong not to shoot when I could
instead of doubting:
if I kill the wolf will I kill every single page
with running rabbits, hiding foxes,
runaway goats, scared weasels,
everything that I love?

21

Muddy shoes tied with two different laces,
a pair of dirty Mickey Mouse socks,
brown trousers grass-stained at the knee,
a belt tightened as for two hands,
a shirt soaked in blood
with many tiny bullet holes,
a loose tie with the image of a mosque
at the bottom,
a pair of broken glasses without the lenses.

That's it.

Where is the man? I screamed.
Where is the man?
I shouted at the Official in clinical attire
piecing together
a nameless skeleton
as if solving a mere puzzle.

*You are not allowed to scream
inside the Forensic Centre,*
the Official's shadow insisted
as he showed me the exit door.

It was the longest walk of my life.

Outside,
summer in the shape of a golden ring
was smiling at me,
as if to an accomplice,
as if nothing had happened,
leaving me with my darkness.

Sometimes people come to the Forensic Centre
and scream after recognizing their own clothes.

Under the innocent sky,
I was left to search for the answer
to a bitter question:
how long will it be before the shoes, socks, pants, belt,
tie, shirt and pair of glasses
find the exit
and I see them walking the street?

22

For you, walking depression
I collect dry November leaves
to extract April's perfume.

You who sit on the corner of our bed
looking through the window
into the gray stomach of a sky
that eats sparrows
and vomits owls.

But it seems you don't see me anymore.
You don't hear the moles gnawing the silence
in the pillows
as I write you dear messages on my skin,
my own blood the neon ink.

The joyful lines of poetry I recite to you
came back to my mouth in the shape
of shrivelled roots of flowers
I planted in your ears long ago
waiting for spring.

Like a tin drum
in an orchestra of violins,
like a horseman on a camel racing
I wave to you with a black scarf
from the starting line
hoping the sun will bleach it white
before the finish.

Before I become ill myself
waiting for November
to start smelling like April.

23

I dedicated myself to studying the enemy
on the other side of the bank.
I read all their books
and burned them
just to warm my feet by the fire.
I enjoyed pretending not to hear the pleas
of fictional characters
begging me to give them a little more time
to get used to ash.
Their proverbs about love,
which we used to cite in teaching our
square-headed pupils not to trust
those round-headed bastard kids across the bank,
screamed in the fire.

I would crank up the radio,
listening to our wordless hymns
cringing at their songs
that shamelessly resemble ours,
I threw the all the enemy's CDs
into the muddy river between us,
and I could hear mute fish singing.

I watched all their films
searching for hidden messages
about the difference between us and them.
Cheap propaganda seeped through the fake tears
of their mothers visiting mass graves.
They must have an enormous budget for makeup,
I laughed to myself,
delighting in
the weathered, colourless flags.

But I couldn't deny the repulsive beauty
of their side of the riverbank,
where future terrorist lovers kiss
under the blue sky
but stare at the stars
on our side.

Even preoccupied with my secret mission,
I wouldn't forget to stop by the daycare
to pick up my children
that I don't have.
I would send flowers to the address
of the darling I don't have
and pick up them up dry the next week.

Only on Christmas Eve would I cry a bit,
raising a champagne toast to the man in uniform
watching me from the mirror
and wondering why my enemy
smiles strangely at me.

24

Children walk backwards to school
shouldering backpacks
full of cement mush,
passing through the fernery
toward teachers who wave to them
with paper shovels.

My kids are not with them.
They are obsessed with life.
Some of them do business with hospitals.
Some of them do business with penitentiaries.
Some of them do business with funeral homes.

The children going to school
wave to me with weeds I harvested
on my concrete balcony.

I love to watch the world from my window.
I planted a rose-bush upside down
believing the roots would rather smell the sky
and the rosebud would rather smell the soil
full of the bones of saints.

My children are self-taught survivors,
palm readers who tell fortunes
only to those without a future.
gambling only with something they don't own.

They used to bury themselves
every morning
after waking up
and running from the mirror
to elude me.

In spring
when weeds blossom
I wonder if my loneliness would be more comfortable
if I taught my children to fly
instead of making gravitation bearable.

Every time the telephone rings
I hope one of them is calling me
to ask
if the rose tree I planted upside down
still blooms.

25

I have tried to write a poem wearing boxing gloves
in the empty ring
in front of the empty chairs.

I get into the empty ring
raising my hands in triumph
thanks to the electrician
leaving the spotlight on a few more minutes,
thanks to the cleaning ladies not
sweeping me off the stage,
thanks to cameramen
letting me see my face frozen on the screen
next to the image of the champion,
thanks to the poor guys from the Employment Centre
who ripped the champion's posters down
after I left the ring.

Then I went home
to sit at the kitchen table and write
the poem about blood and sweat,
about bruises that only I feel,
the poem in which I give thanks to no one.

Except my nightingale
who flutters every time he sees me
and waits patiently for me to take off the gloves
to feed him.

26

My first pair of glasses
my parents forced me to wear
to see people better.
A sniper's binoculars were installed
in the deer antler frames
and I recognized in people
what I didn't want to see,
too big for childish eyes,
seeing people as deer
or as hunters.

My second pair of glasses, with flashlight lenses,
my teachers forced me to wear to help me
find the invisible.

I didn't like them.
Usually the recommended books were written
by the hunters
and between the lines I would read the testimony of deer.

The third pair of glasses
I made myself.
Into a plastic frame I inserted
simple window glass
to see myself better.

I didn't like that pair either.
Every time I wore them
I saw one half of me as a hunter
the other half as a deer.

Now,
half blind I walk the streets clumsy
bumping into passers-by
and apologize politely,
explaining that I just lost my last pair of glasses,
a minute ago
on my way home.
Celebrating for not seeing them
in the shape of hunters
or deer.

27

Because of you,
I miss my bus stop and I am still wandering
looking for my way back.
I fall asleep in one country listening to scouts
singing your name
and wake up on a train station bench
in the next country
where the flag's designer never heard of you.

The wind is my witness
I never even thought of giving up my search
looking for you.
the engineers even have different ideas
about which way you went.

Empty fizzy-drink cans still shake the same way
when trains blow into the station.
It's not the same station I came from,
it's not the same wind I went with,
not the same me.

28

Oh, how wonderful is to be protected by bars.
The prison cell opened automatically for me
when I started to sing heedless of rhymes and refrains.
I locked myself up to get some peace
as I tried to rhyme myself
with the photo in my passport.

Through the keyhole I could hear how the wind sings
like the judge who sentenced me.
all the holes in the cell's wall
are the throats
of those who used to sing with me
in the same choir.
I know they still think of me.

But they are different now
watching the prison from the other side
of the bars.
They see how psychiatrists patrol the streets
singing military songs.
Behind them monks with snow on their sandals
who crawl offering winning tickets for ballots
to those in a long line at the cash machine.
to those whose legs smell like olive oil
whose fingers smell like cocaine.

Even my children on their way to school
sing a song celebrating natives,
songs glorifying invaders.

The whole city is singing.
Only the nightingales are silent
with me, looking through the bars.
Only the spider I inherited
in the corner of my cell
knows what am I thinking.
It's a pity
just a few people outside
try to learn the language of spiders.
www.languageofspiders.com

29

I retired my soldiers, victorious liberators,
sent them home as heroes with their guns,
and sleeping pills as their only ammunition.

I bought the house on the border of the city
we were fighting with
till yesterday,
hanging all my medals in the windows
and starting a business making table lamps
out of turtle armour.

Business is going well. It would be more successful
if so many people weren't getting killed in car accidents
caused by my ex-soldiers.

Because of them
the city police shut down the bars
and open up the jail cells on Friday,
because of them surgeons work overtime
knitting goblins on my soldiers' proud faces,
because of them even their children sleep at
relatives' houses on Sunday
to avoid watching their fathers trying to hang themselves
again and again.

On Monday I turn off my telephone
because my ex-soldiers will call me about the hunger strike
over their small pensions.

The citizens who until yesterday forced their children
to jump into the liberator's uniform
now claim that the schoolbooks' passages about patriotism
reek of alcohol, sperm and blood.
The new pupils spend most of their pocket money on perfume.
Peace became too expensive for the city
that used to manufacture so many warriors.

I've heard the mayor announce that Parliament
will buy a huge number of my turtle lamps
despite complaints from the neighbouring city's mayor
that peace looks lame.
That idiot
who forced his own retired soldiers to get a sex change
has whined for years about the stench
of decomposing turtles
in my backyard.
I don't mind why not a single newspaper dares
to take up the issue.

I sit on my private hill of dead turtles
who believed they would find eternity
just because of their suit of armour.
I drink my morning coffee
with a loaded gun in the sugar jar,
in a neatly pressed uniform
waiting for the telephone to ring.

30

Tonight my bean soup burned
while I was busy at the kitchen table
writing about those bastard poets
who refuse to write about the universe
just because they have unfinished business
here on earth.
refusing to grow up.

I drew a picture of a peacock on an armoured car
but it didn't even notice when the machine gun
sprayed bullets toward the chicken farm.
In the cherished garden
I put up a billboard with a new politician on it
announcing winds of change.
A few years later the billboard is still there
but moles are the neglected garden's only visitors.
I sent my well-groomed dog
who brought me newspapers for years
to fetch me a picture book
and he never came back.

I wrote everything
with a clever pen on a dull white sheet
and I didn't like the way the words responded.
I started loving it when in rage
I blotted out the lines and dragged my index finger
across every picture
to get a bleary mash of grey clouds.

Now I am sitting at the kitchen table trying to eat
burned bean soup
pretending it's the taste I've always preferred
if only to spite the army of chefs who,
with a peacock under the arm
and a picture book in their hands,
wait for their share of the universe.

31

What a fool I was believing I could buy eternity.
After I got rich,
before Death knocked at my door,
I purchased the soul of a poor man
promising to feed him as long as he lives
if he would die for me when the time comes.
Soon he moved his bed into the kitchen
next to the fridge
because he got too fat to walk upstairs to his room.

I paid good money to the terminally ill man
for his soul
promising to pay his medical bills
till he offered his last breath in place of mine.
Recently he gave me a notice about healthy living and
a new generation of smart pills
before leaving to play basketball.

Today,
when I came home
exhausted by endless meetings
with the bankruptcy lawyer and mortgage clerks
those two dying men refused to open the door.
Through the keyhole they told me
that I looked too pale and sick to let in.
Like Death.
God forbid.

32

If I were not a poet I would be an historian
a cold-blooded eunuch contemplating beauty,
my fingers on the calculator
adding up what there is to gain
instead of realizing what I am missing.

But once you marry poetry
you get the space between the lines
to breathe.

Acknowledgements

My thanks to all those dear friends and writers who have helped to make my Bosnian-Serbo-Croatian English look more English. Special thanks to Amela Marin, Susan Sontag, Fraser Sutherland, Tom Simpson and Colin Carberry, to everyone who encouraged me to write in English, and to my friend Gerda Stevenson for introducing me to Smokestack Books.